A Book of Hours

Meredith Hooper

Cambridge Reading

General Editors
Richard Brown and Kate Ruttle

Consultant Editor
Jean Glasberg

PUBLISHED BY THE PRESS SYNDICATE OF THE UNIVERSITY OF CAMBRIDGE
The Pitt Building, Trumpington Street, Cambridge CB2 1RP, United Kingdom

CAMBRIDGE UNIVERSITY PRESS
The Edinburgh Building, Cambridge CB2 2RU, United Kingdom
40 West 20th Street, New York, NY 10011-4211, USA
10 Stamford Road, Oakleigh, Melbourne 3166, Australia

First published 1997

Printed in the United Kingdom at the University Press, Cambridge

Typeset in Concorde and Infant Clairvaux

A catalogue record for this book is available from the British Library

ISBN 0 521 49840 6 paperback

Picture research: Maureen Cowdroy

Acknowledgements
The author wishes to acknowledge the invaluable assistance of Janet Backhouse,
Curator of Illuminated Manuscripts, The British Library, in the research and writing
of this book.

The publishers are grateful to the following for permission to reproduce photographs:
page 4 self-portrait of Simon Bening, reproduced by courtesy of the Board of
Trustees of the Victoria and Albert Museum (museum no. P. 159 – 1910); **page 5**
copyright Bibliothèque Royale Albert 1er, Brussels (MS. 9278-80, fol. 10r); **page 6**
Mary of Burgundy, copyright Austrian National Library, Vienna (E 5422 – C[D]
COD. 1857, fol. 14v).

Pages of the 'Golf Book' reproduced by courtesy of the British Library Board. Add.
MS 24098: **pages 8 and 9** f.18v. and f.19r.; **pages 10 and 11** f.19v. and f. 20r.; **pages
12 and 13** f.20v. and f.21r.; **pages 14 and 15** f.21v. and f.22r.; **pages 16 and 17**
f.22v. and f.23r.; **pages 18 and 19** f.23v. and f.24r.; **pages 20 and 21** (and page 7)
f.24v. and f.25r.; **pages 22 and 23** f.25v. and f.26r.; **pages 24 and 25** f.26v. and f.27r.;
pages 26 and 27 f.27v. and f.28r.; **pages 28 and 29** f.28v. and f.29r.; **pages 30 and 31**
f.29v. and f.30r.

Contents

The Golf Book

Simon Bening was a famous artist. He painted pictures onto the pages of books. These books were made by hand, so no two books were exactly the same.

Rich customers came to Simon Bening's workshop and asked him to make them books. They looked at paintings in Simon's workshop. Then they chose the paintings which they wanted him to copy into their books. They also chose the words which they wanted in the books.

Simon Bening painted this picture of himself when he was seventy-five. He is holding his glasses in his hand. He lived nearly five hundred years ago in the city of Bruges, which is now in Belgium.

People who were skilled in writing were called 'scribes'. A scribe sat at a desk, copying the words for the new book out of an old book.

Then artists drew patterns and borders on the pages, decorating them with bright colours.

Other artists copied the pictures that the customers had chosen. Simon Bening painted some of the important pictures.

One of the books made in Simon Bening's workshop is called the 'Golf Book' because there is a painting inside it of a game that looks like golf.

The Golf Book was once part of a much longer book, called a Book of Hours. Books of Hours were personal prayer books which were very popular five hundred years ago. Many men and women wanted to say their prayers every day, and Books of Hours gave them the right prayers to say on each day of the year and at different times of the day. A Book of Hours was the only book that many men and women owned.

There are many different kinds of Books of Hours. Ordinary people had plain ones. Rich people had beautiful ones with paintings by famous artists. This lady is holding her Book of Hours very carefully.

This is the actual size of the pages in the Golf Book.

Books of Hours always began with a calendar. The calendar helped people to know which prayers to say on each day. Every month, there were special days when people said special prayers.

The Golf Book has a painting and a list of days and dates for each month of the year. The paintings show men and women at work and enjoying themselves. Some paintings show children playing games. People liked looking at pictures of everyday life, as well as at religious pictures.

8

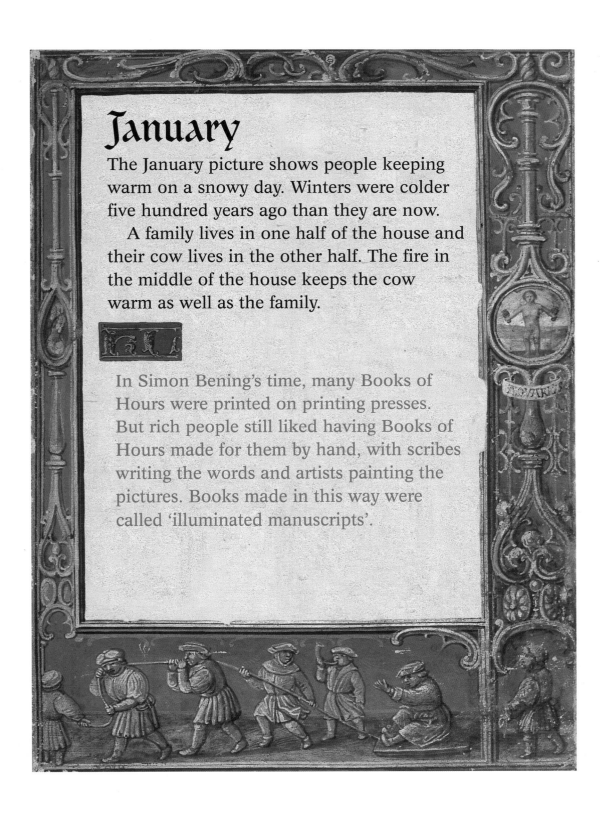

January

The January picture shows people keeping warm on a snowy day. Winters were colder five hundred years ago than they are now.

A family lives in one half of the house and their cow lives in the other half. The fire in the middle of the house keeps the cow warm as well as the family.

In Simon Bening's time, many Books of Hours were printed on printing presses. But rich people still liked having Books of Hours made for them by hand, with scribes writing the words and artists painting the pictures. Books made in this way were called 'illuminated manuscripts'.

10

February

A rich man and his wife are having a feast. People are entertaining them with music and dancing. A big fire is burning in the fireplace, but the rich man and his wife are still wearing fur to keep themselves warm.

The door on the right leads to the kitchen. The door on the left leads outside. Poor people are peeping in. They will get the left-over food at the end of the meal.

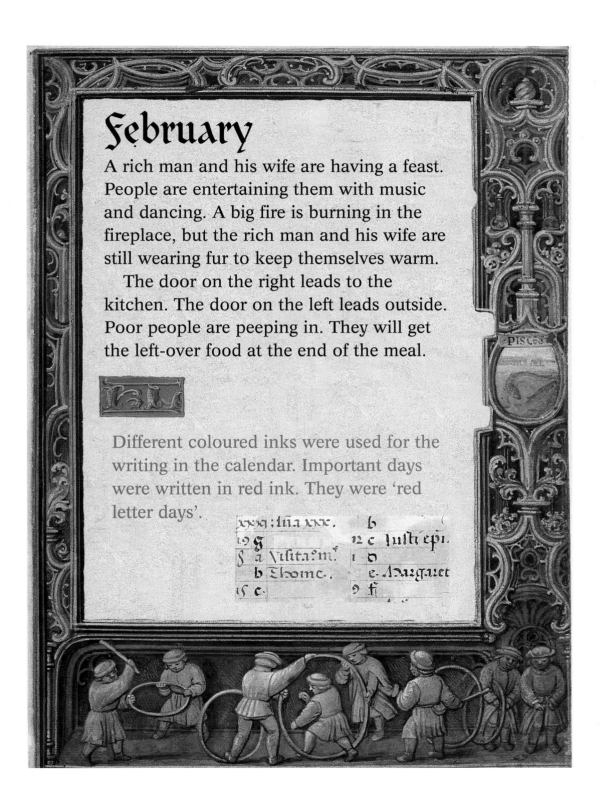

Different coloured inks were used for the writing in the calendar. Important days were written in red ink. They were 'red letter days'.

12

March

A lot of work needs to be done in the garden after the winter. The fence is broken. The herb garden needs to be dug. The lady is telling the gardener what to do. The woodcutters are cutting down a tree which is dying.

The pages of the Golf Book are made of 'vellum', which is made from animal skins. Vellum is thin, soft, white, and so strong that it can last for a thousand years.

Lines were ruled on the pages so that the scribes would know where to write and the artists would know where to draw.

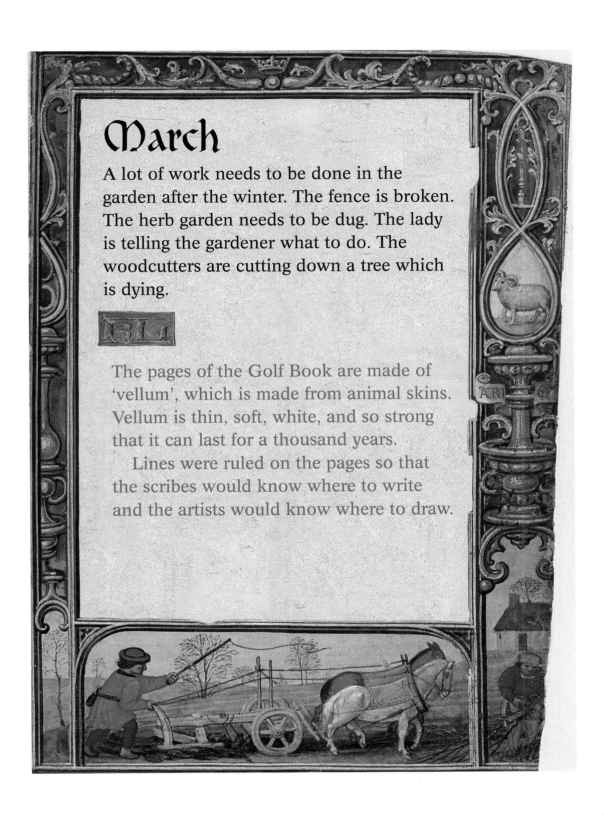

14

April

Spring has come and the rich man and his wife are in the garden with their two children. The man has his hawk on his wrist. The servants are wearing a uniform of yellow jackets and red hats. They must stay outside the garden, behind the fence.

Two storks have built a nest on the chimney of the house.

Scribes worked at sloping desks. They had a pile of sharpened pens made from feathers, and little pots of thick black and red ink to dip their pens into. The words were copied from other Books of Hours, which were propped up high so that they were easy to read. Scribes worked fast and it was easy to make mistakes.

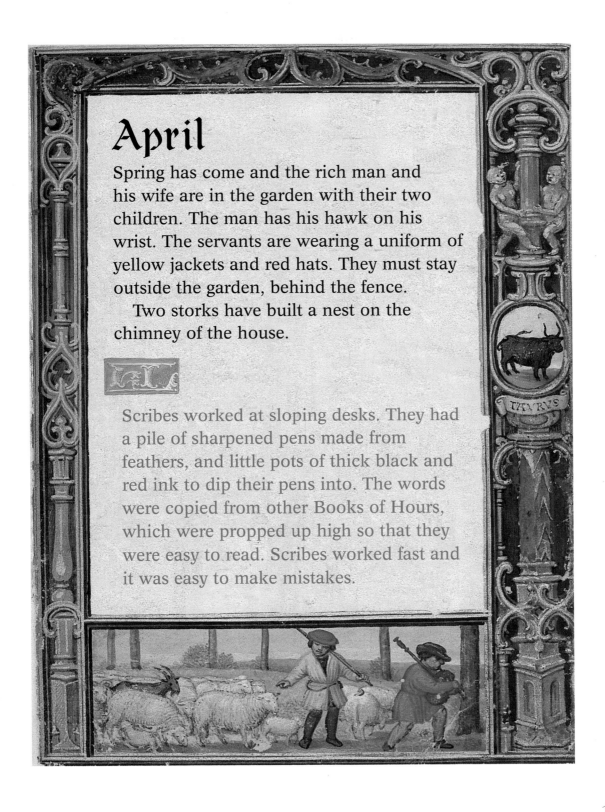

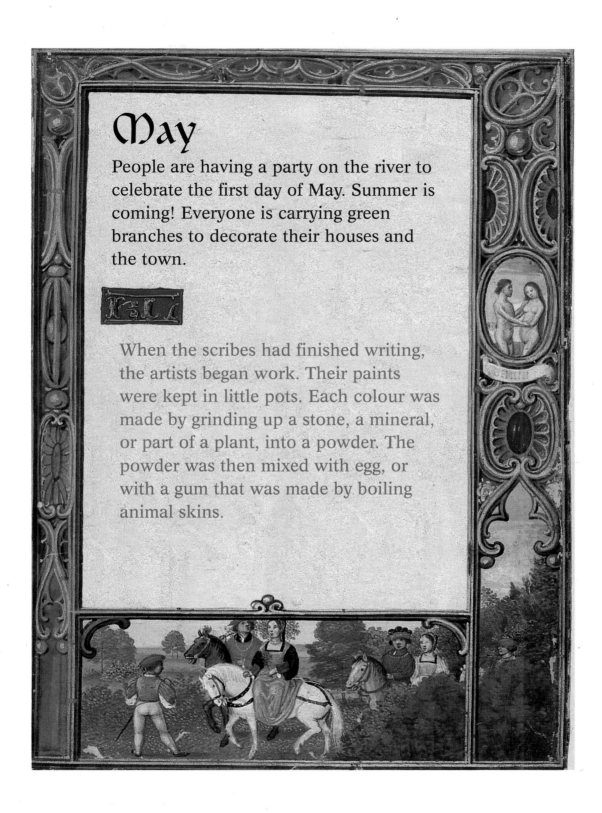

May

People are having a party on the river to celebrate the first day of May. Summer is coming! Everyone is carrying green branches to decorate their houses and the town.

When the scribes had finished writing, the artists began work. Their paints were kept in little pots. Each colour was made by grinding up a stone, a mineral, or part of a plant, into a powder. The powder was then mixed with egg, or with a gum that was made by boiling animal skins.

18

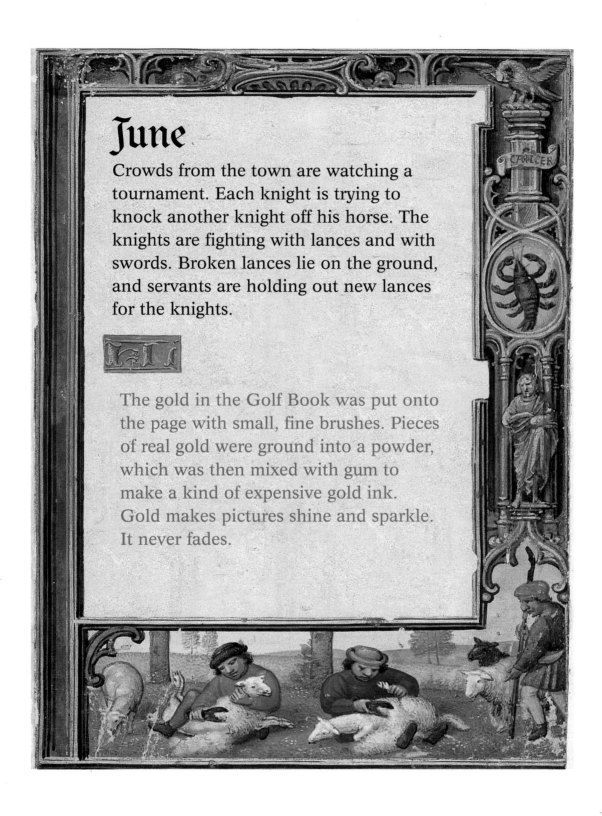

June

Crowds from the town are watching a tournament. Each knight is trying to knock another knight off his horse. The knights are fighting with lances and with swords. Broken lances lie on the ground, and servants are holding out new lances for the knights.

The gold in the Golf Book was put onto the page with small, fine brushes. Pieces of real gold were ground into a powder, which was then mixed with gum to make a kind of expensive gold ink. Gold makes pictures shine and sparkle. It never fades.

July

In summer, men and women cut the long grass to make into hay.

The rich man is going hunting with his hawks. He is riding a pony. One hawk is sitting on his left wrist. His servants are carrying the other two hawks.

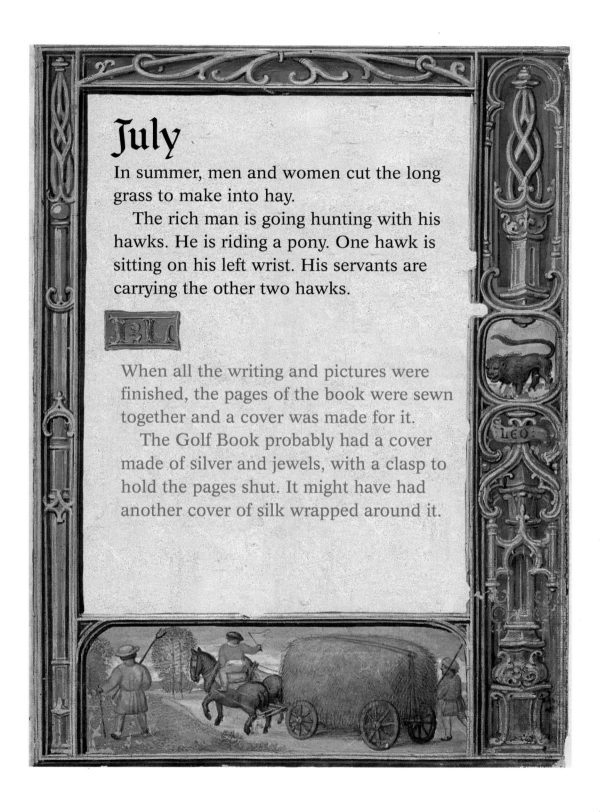

When all the writing and pictures were finished, the pages of the book were sewn together and a cover was made for it.

The Golf Book probably had a cover made of silver and jewels, with a clasp to hold the pages shut. It might have had another cover of silk wrapped around it.

22

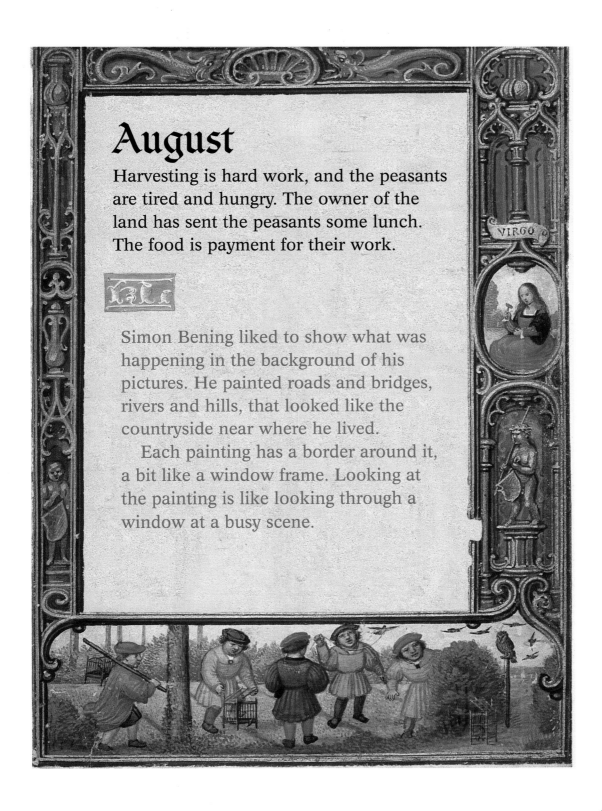

August

Harvesting is hard work, and the peasants are tired and hungry. The owner of the land has sent the peasants some lunch. The food is payment for their work.

Simon Bening liked to show what was happening in the background of his pictures. He painted roads and bridges, rivers and hills, that looked like the countryside near where he lived.

Each painting has a border around it, a bit like a window frame. Looking at the painting is like looking through a window at a busy scene.

VIRGO

24